UNWRITINGS
A Journey into Visual Poetry

by Laura Ortiz

Cover art by Laura Ortiz

© 2021 Laura Ortiz
All Rights Reserved

ISBN: 978-1-7348662-4-7

Post-Asemic Press 015

postasemicpress.wordpress.com
Contact: postasemicpress@gmail.com
postasemicpress.blogspot.com

Unwritings

"Ditaturiore quiam faciatur magnam volessu ntibusapel et liquunt eatet aliquo experruptisi sape perferest la consera tionsec estiandita volest, si comnis alia qui officiet laborro…"

Unwritings

Laura Ortiz' Unwritings opens with her own introduction written in a kind of false Latin interspersed with other apocryphal languages, a great opening for a book in which possible archaic languages are suggested in a strongly visual context. Her introduction, however, is not completely without sense: "Ditaturiore quiam faciatur magnam volessu ntibusapel et liquunt eatet aliquo experruptisi sape perferest la consera tionsec estiandita volest, si comnis alia qui officiet laborro...", which seems to be commentary about the type of writing she is interested in. Her works in the book are a melding of visual poetry, holographic abstract writing, drawing, and drawn writing. The result, rather than appearing to be a creation of fake archaic documents, is a very contemporary visual art, that includes writing as a kind of atmosphere, a colorant that adds an important depth or explanation to the overall impact, in that handwriting in itself is expressive of meaning, quite apart from any lexical content it might (or might not) have. It is no surprise that this Argentine/Canadian poet is associated with the international INI group and movement. Her work here, deeply colorful and unique, has a strong transcultural and translinguistic appeal. I look forward to seeing more of Laura Ortiz' work!.

Dr. John M. Bennett

Unwritings

One of the many qualities of Laura Ortiz's visual work is her multiplication of graphic layers into a complex sequencing. Her Unwritings create an anti- or hyper- semantic environment, which brings to mind the construction of perspectives / architecture. One isn't sure if their eye is drawn to the quasi-texts or to the abstract lines and areas of color.

At the same time, these multi-layered interventions seem to be superpositions and overlapped strata forming a kind of coexisting drawings, or if you will, whose identity cannot be reduced to a single (restrictive) definition. No one side seems to prevail and assume the role of the first "code" on the page. All of them contribute to the overall impact that the piece has on the reader.

If one of the INI's poetics statements describes "densely packed arrangements of letters, words, glyphs, and symbols" where often "images and abstract shapes are superposed", it can definitely be said that most of the experiments Ortiz is practicing since (at least) the year 2016 ---up to now go in that direction. And she's perfectly aware of it, as her afterword states.

The pages that are filled with single glyphs or waterfalls of simple intertwined signs bring our imagination to extremely far regions: maybe times past. When/where some letters appear to have an Etruscan impact we may see the cultural heritage of some Western civilizations. (And a kind of "legacy feeling" in the vast aesthetic field, too.)

Chessboards, orbits, dialogues between impossible languages, between volumes that face each other, and circles that recall Kriwet's alphabets, invite us to and lead us through a journey. That journey is both inside (but also outside!); series of signs which paradoxically appear to be alien because they're actually deeply rooted in our mind.

Marco Giovenale

Unwritings

Unwritings

Unwritings

Unwritings

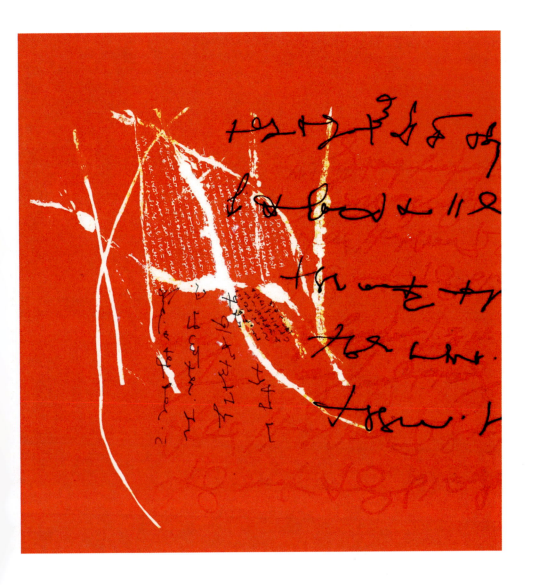

Unwritings

Unwritings

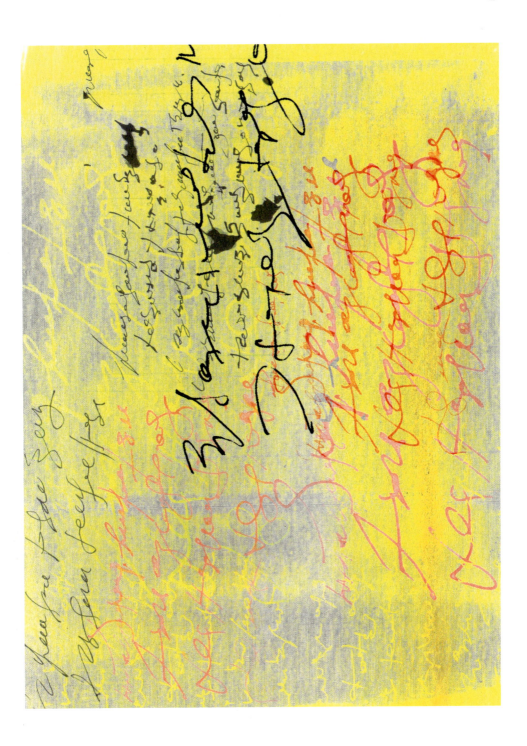

Unwritings

Unwritings

Unwritings

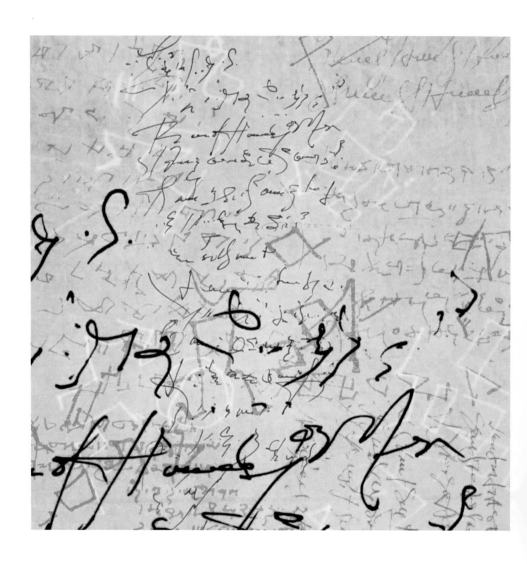

Unwritings

Unwritings

Unwritings

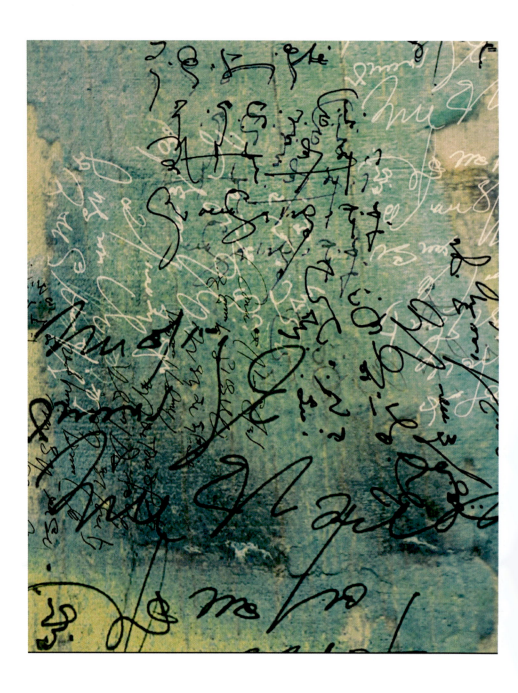

Unwritings

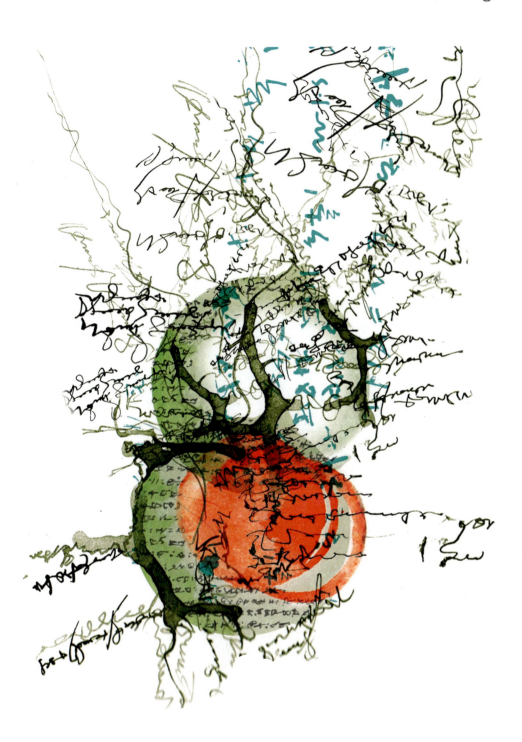

Unwritings

Unwritings

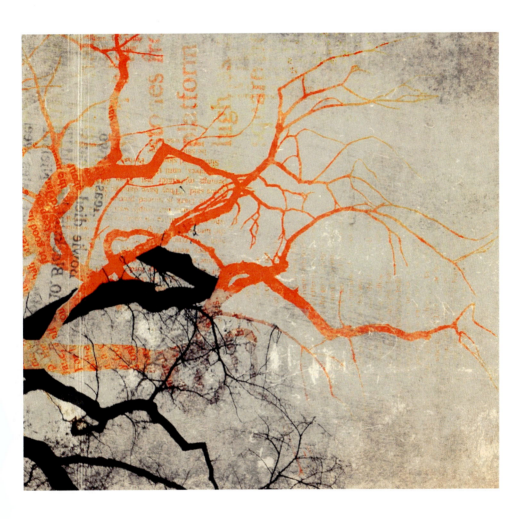

Unwritings

Unwritings

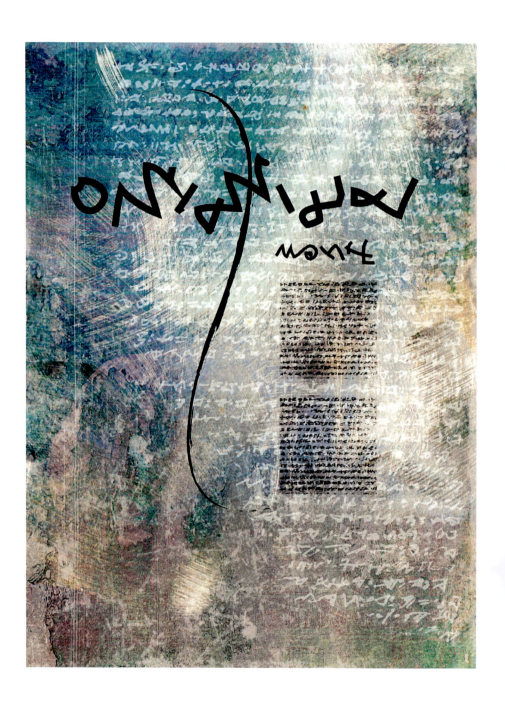

Unwritings

Unwritings

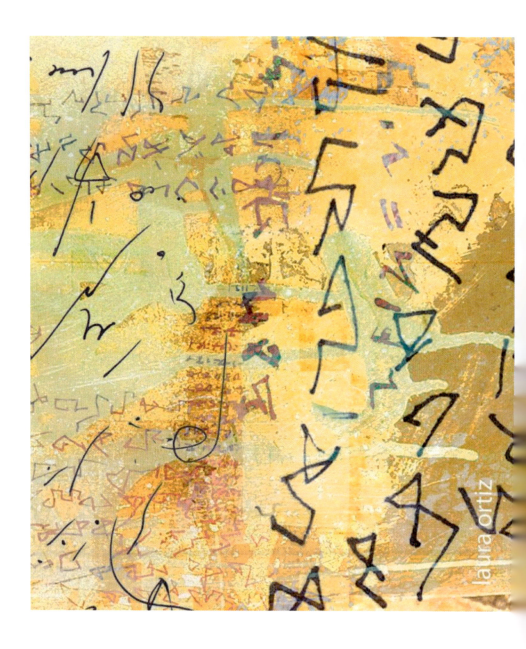

Unwritings

Unwritings

Unwritings

Unwritings

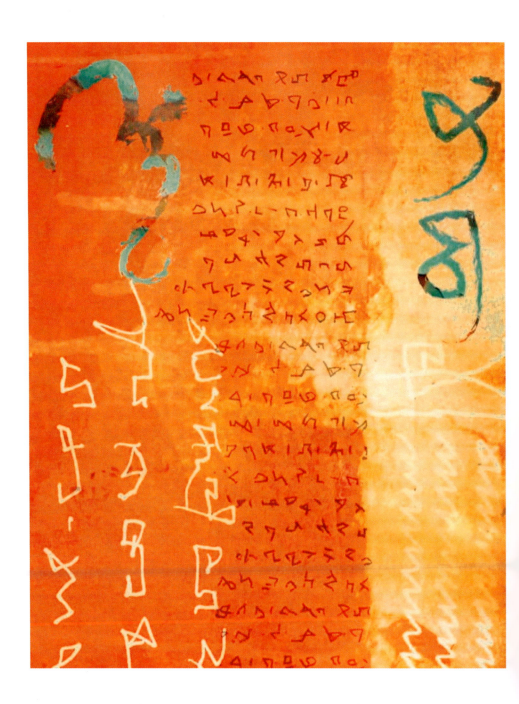

Unwritings

Unwritings

Unwritings

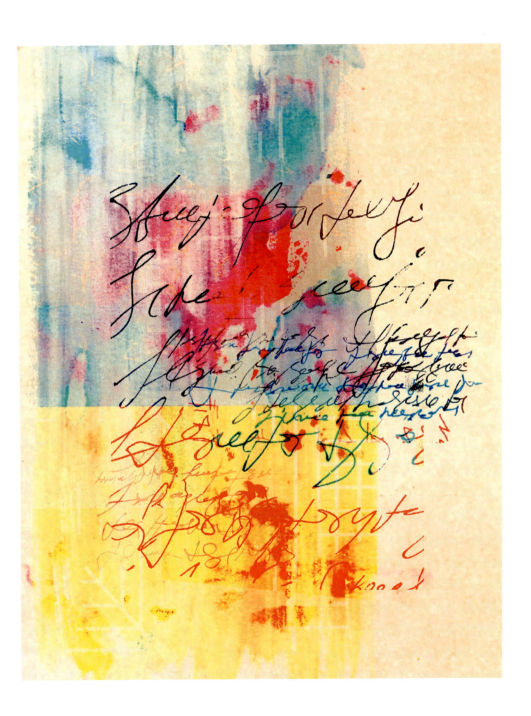

Unwritings

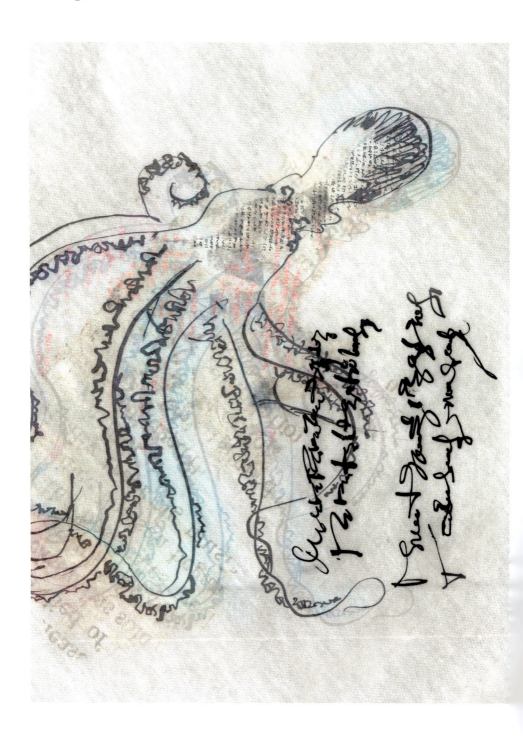

Unwritings

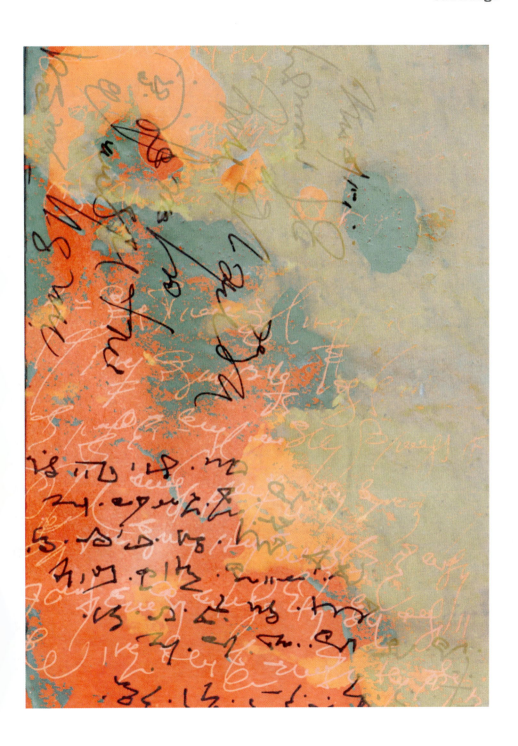

Unwritings

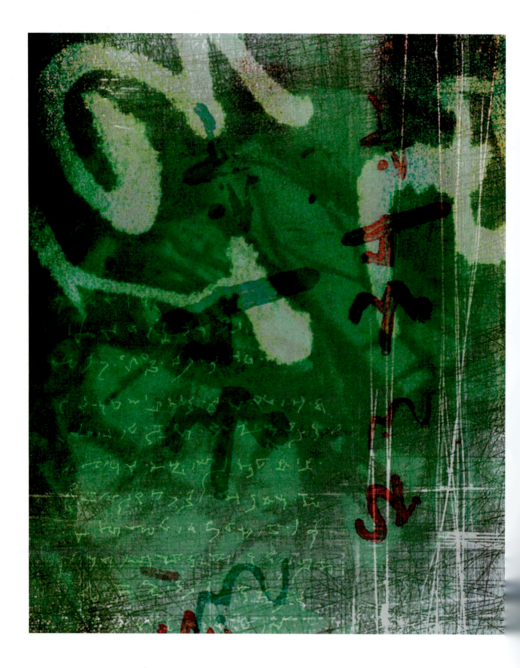

Unwritings

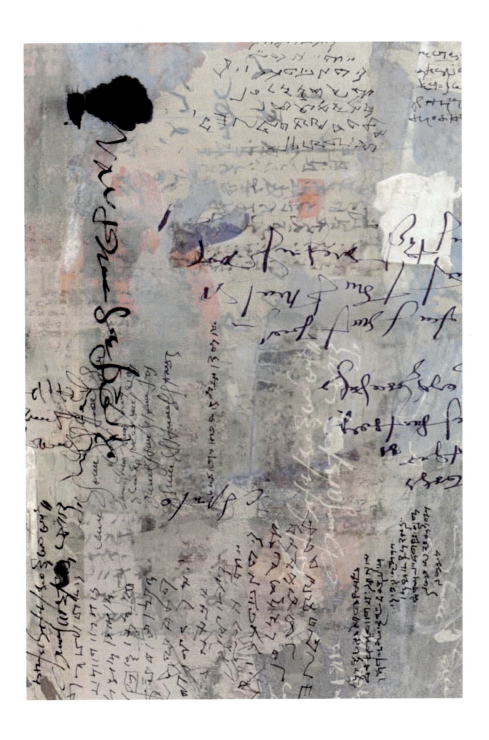

Unwritings

Unwritings

Unwritings

Unwritings

Unwritings

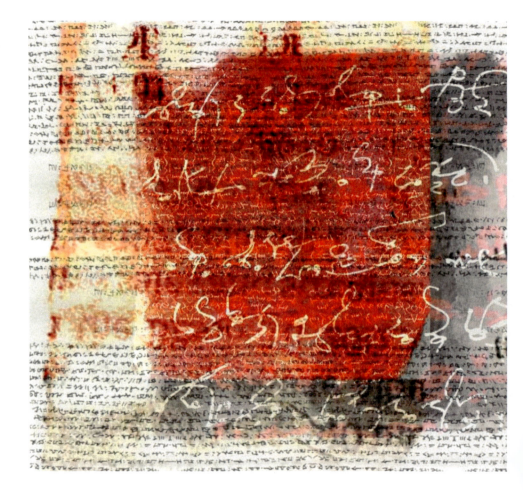

Unwritings

Unwritings

Unwritings

Unwritings

Unwritings

Unwritings

Unwritings

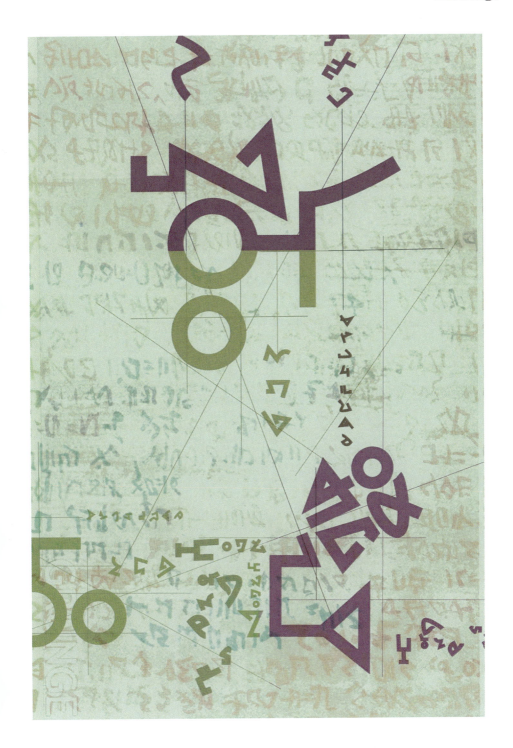

49

Unwritings

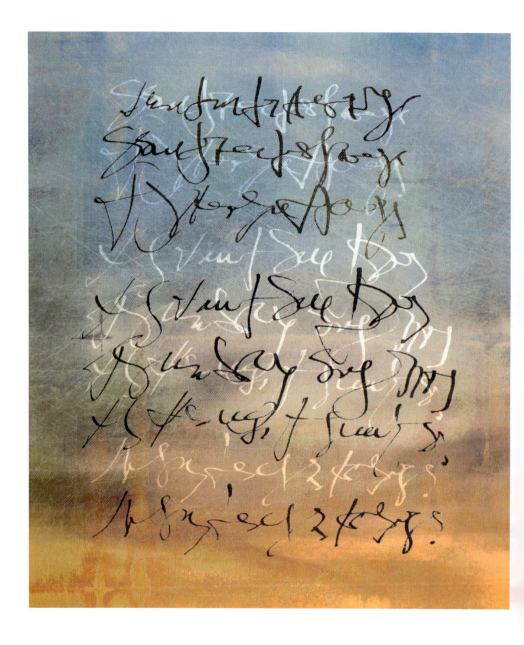

Unwritings

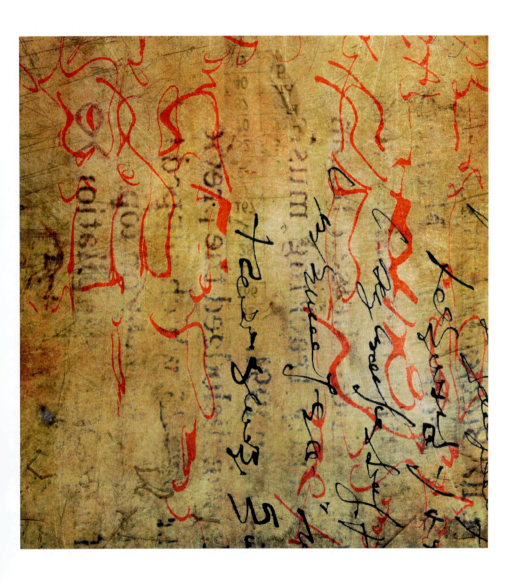

Unwritings

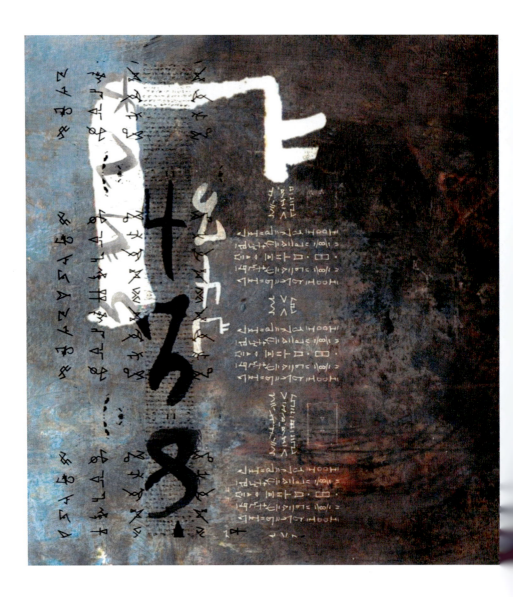

Unwritings

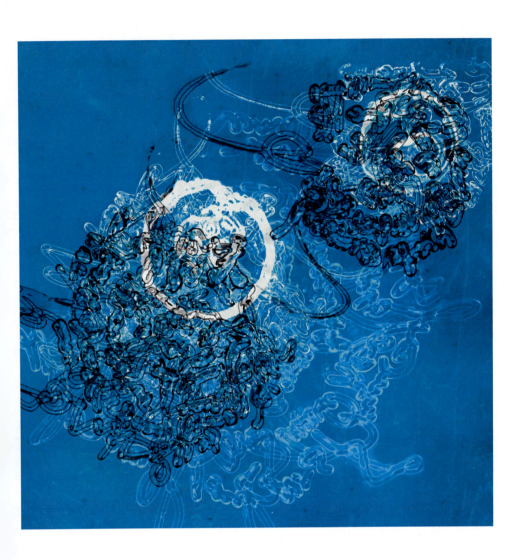

Unwritings

Unwritings

Unwritings

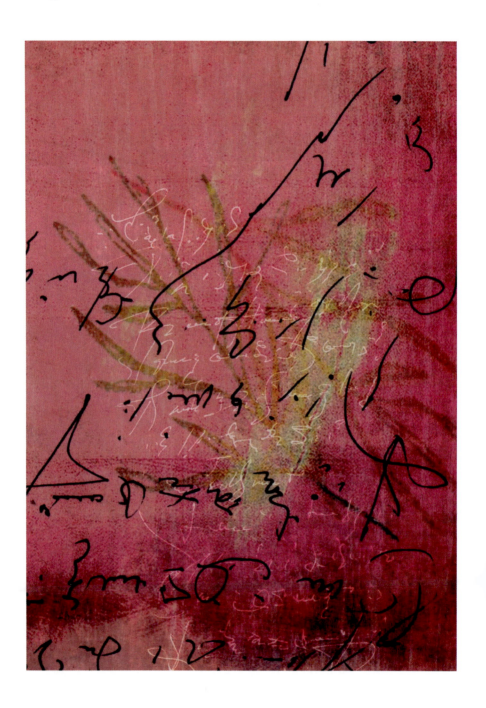

Unwritings

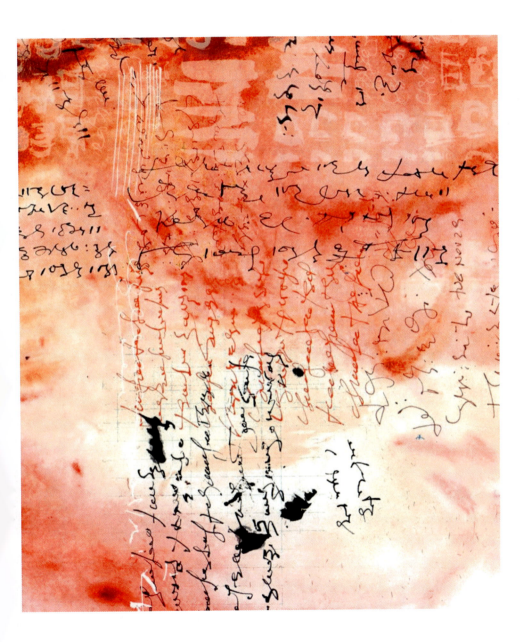

Unwritings

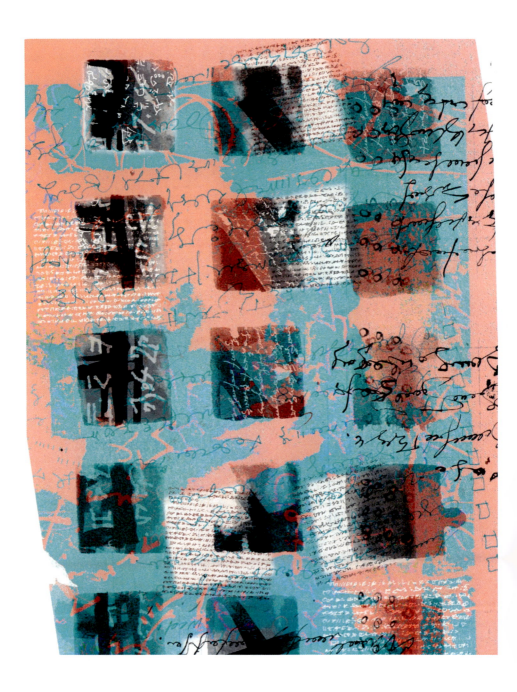

Unwritings

Unwritings

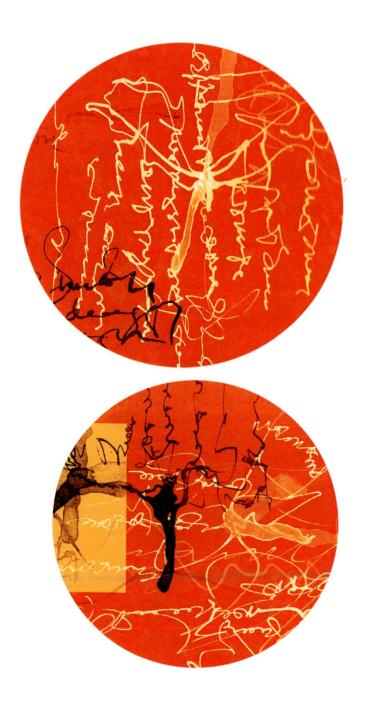

Unwritings

Unwritings

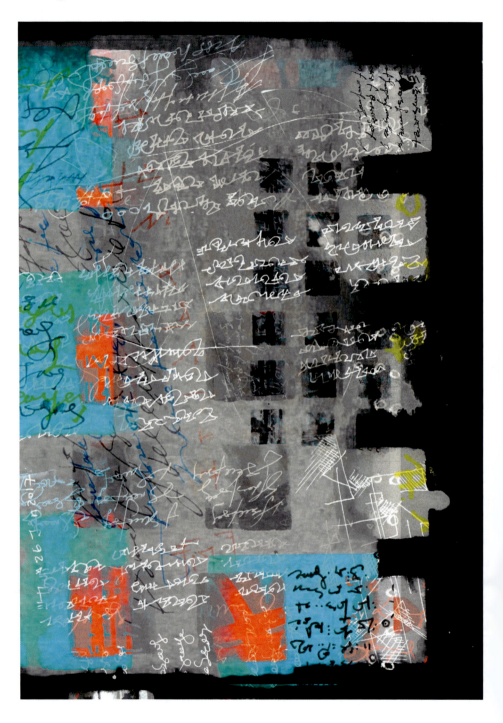

Unwritings

Unwritings

Unwritings

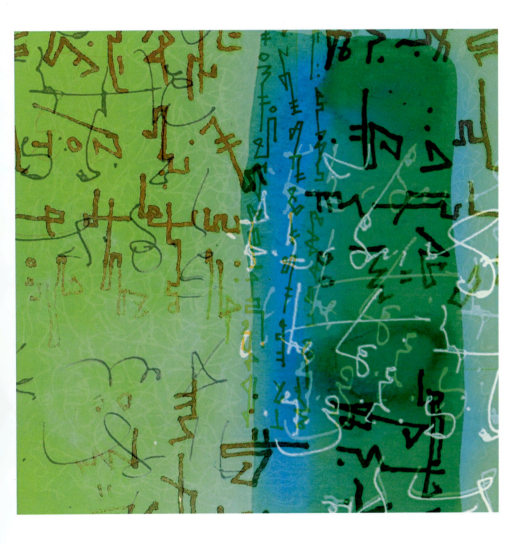

Unwritings

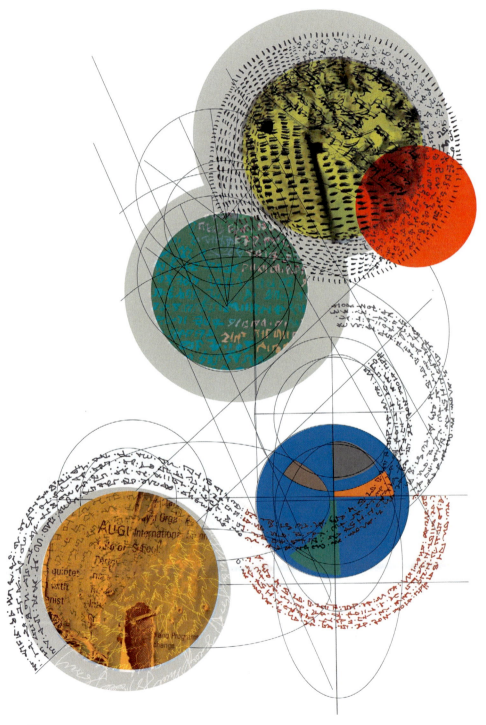

Unwritings

Unwritings

Unwritings

Unwritings

Unwritings

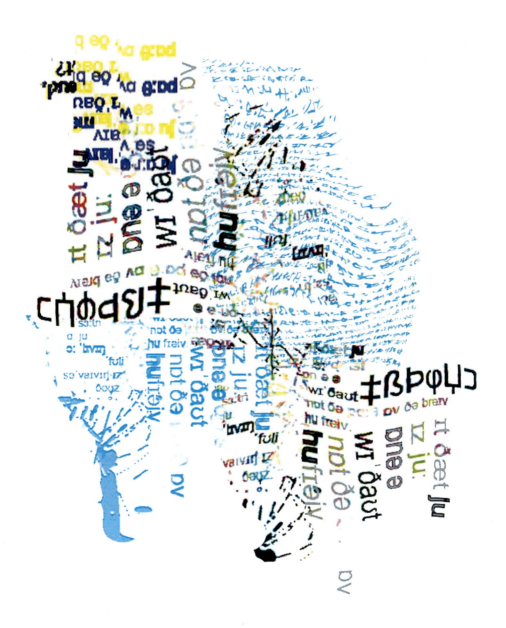

Unwritings

Unwritings

Unwritings

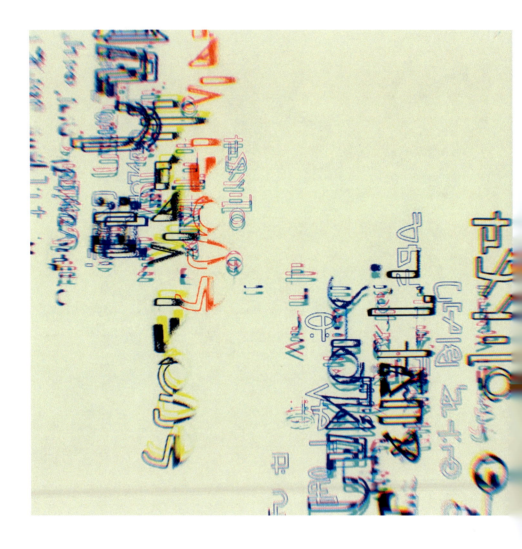

Unwritings

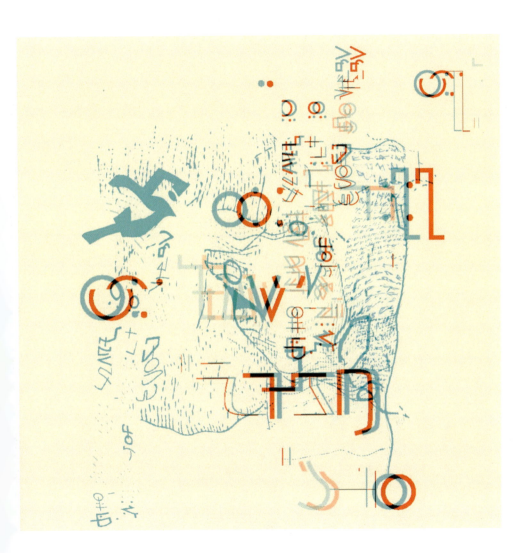

Unwritings

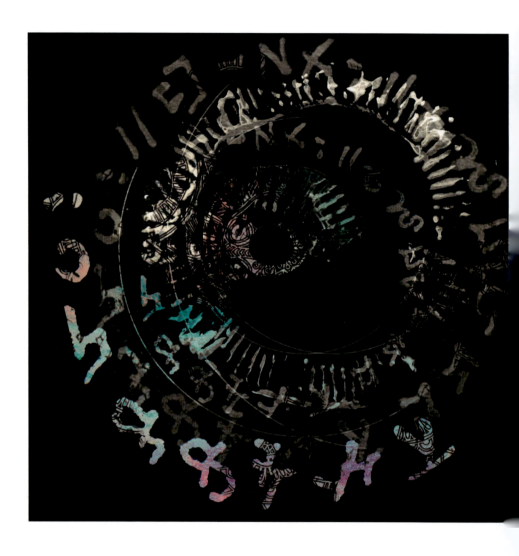

Unwritings

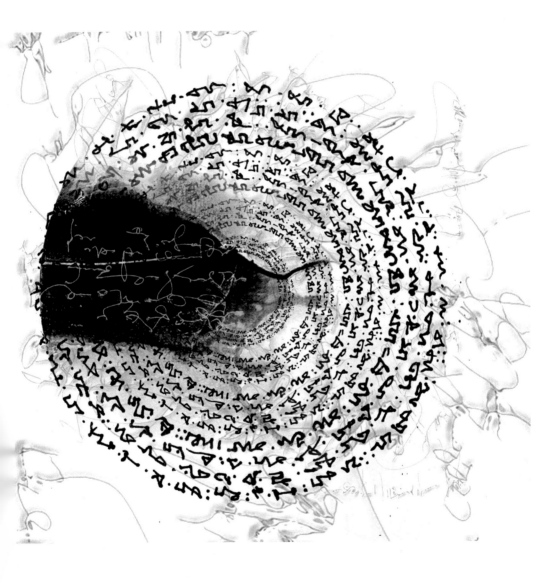

Unwritings

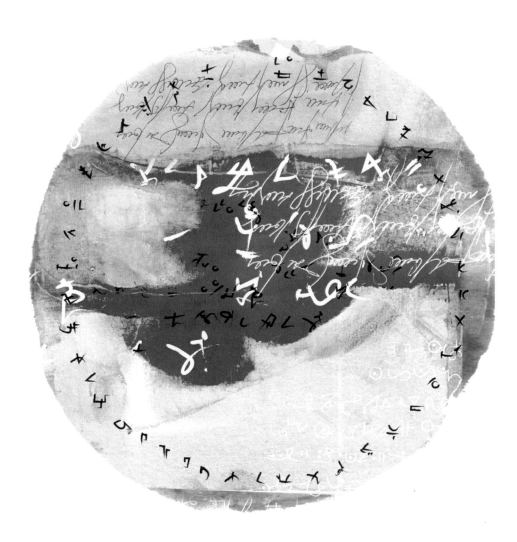

Unwritings

Unwritings

Unwritings

Unwritings

Unwritings

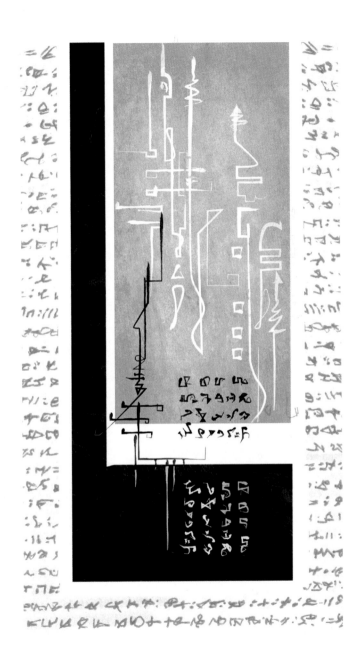

Unwritings

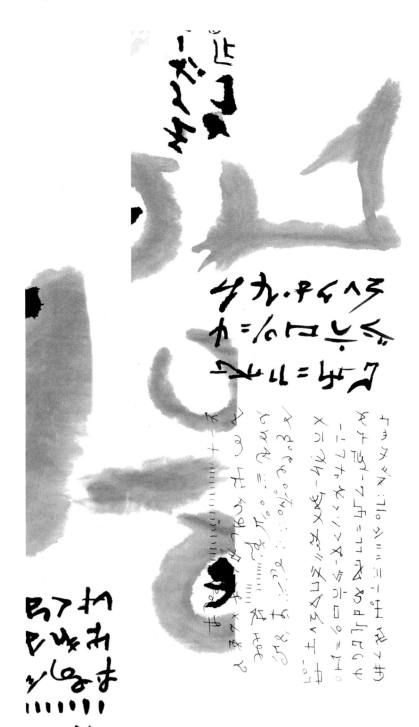

Unwritings

Unwritings

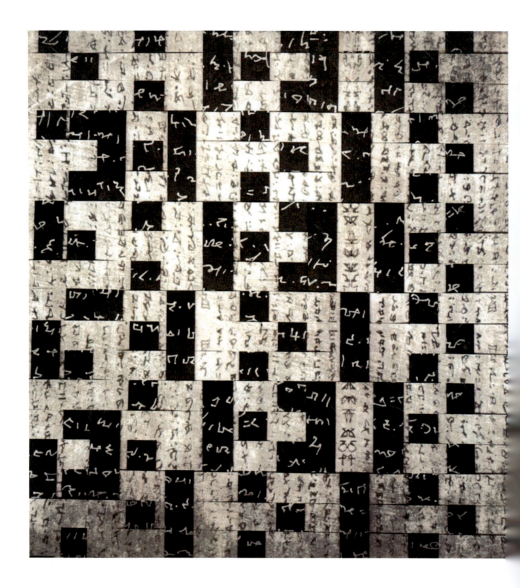

Unwritings

Unwritings

Unwritings

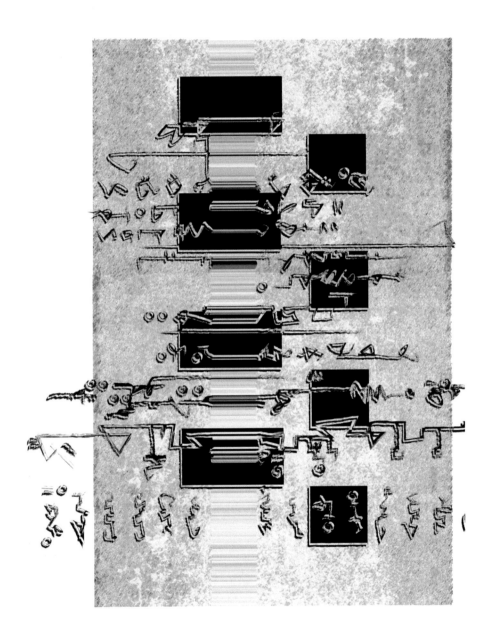

Unwritings

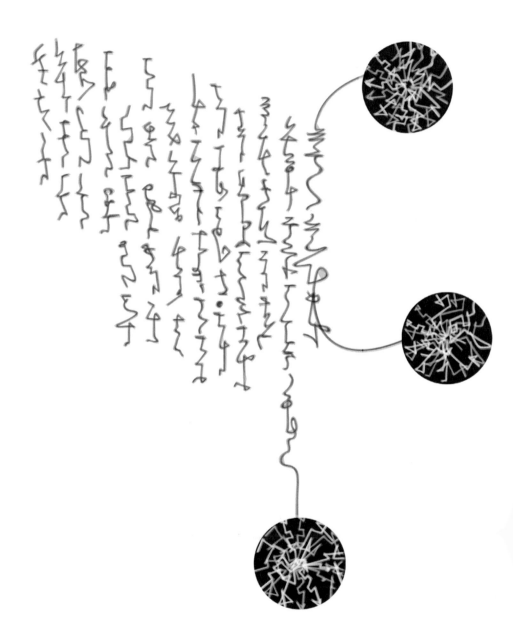

Unwritings

Unwritings

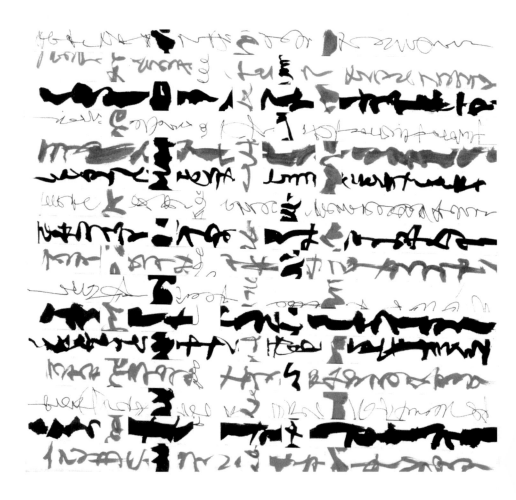

Unwritings

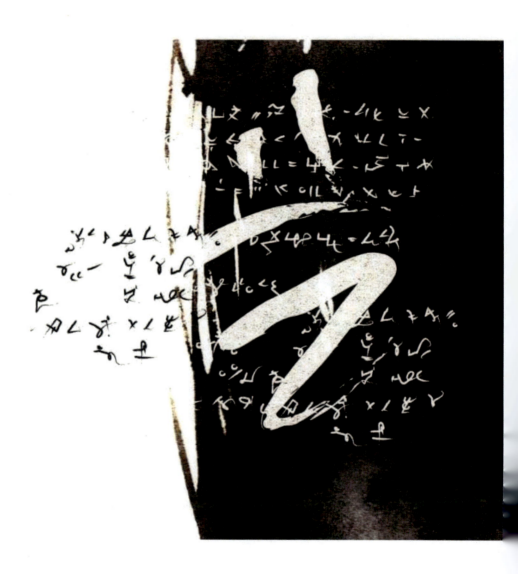

Unwritings

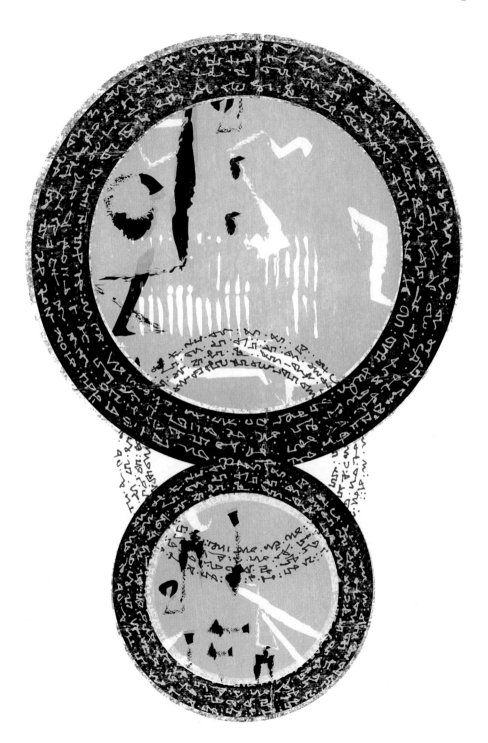

Unwritings

Unwritings

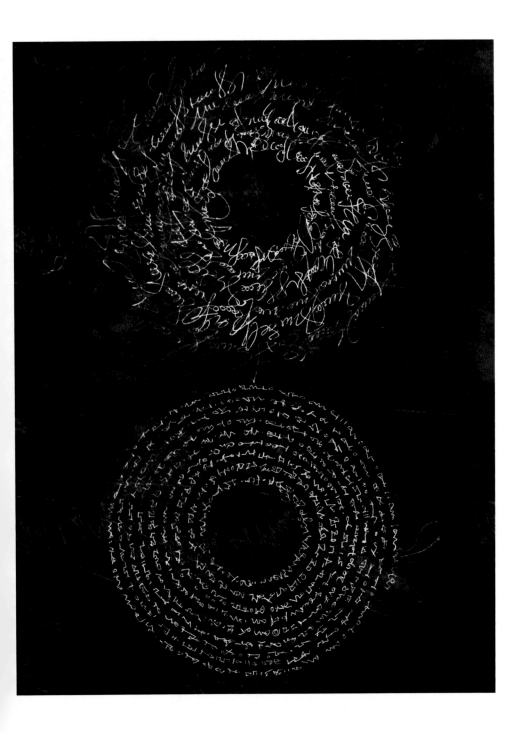

Unwritings

Unwritings

Unwritings: A Journey to Visual Poetry presents my multidimensional visual poetry artwork from 2016 to 2021. It tells the visual story of my quest of self-discovery as an artist, which I have traveled in the company of artistic communities such as INI, Asemic, Fluxus, Dada, Pop Art, and Trashpo, as well as practitioners of concrete, and visual poetry.

Having grown up under the influence of native South American and European cultures, I have always been very interested in languages, symbols, and cultures. As a child, I used to pay close attention to my father's work in advertising as he painted, drew, and designed.

When I finished a graphic design program in 2011 and moved to Canada, I started approaching images in an artistic manner, producing pieces that flourished and continued developing while I joined the aforementioned artistic communities, who have received my works openly and warmly.

It has been a long journey filled with joy and challenges. I have pushed myself to produce works with quality and originality through experimentation and different media, including ink, oil, acrylic, pencils, markers, and software. I have always sought to learn more each time to give each piece a new dimensional layer of creativity and aesthetic communication.

As its creator is a member of the international avant-garde movement INISMO, each visual piece featured in this book displays a multidimensional treatment through the interaction of layers of colors, geometric shapes, photography, and automatic and composed symbolic language, saturating it with mysterious, mystic, arcane meanings. Automatic calligraphic writings, symbolic writings and visual elements interact with each other to create new itineraries of meanings, sometimes evoking the hieroglyphs from ancient cultures, past and present language systems of aboriginal civilizations, Chinese and Japanese characters, present spiritual esoteric systems of belief and practice, or the world itself, which is always evolving and changing.

Unwritings

Many of these works have been featured in exhibitions at contemporary art venues around the world, such as Asemic Writing Exhibition Mappature del Contemporaneo at Parco Archeologico in Scolaciumin, Italy; Concreta-Fetapoesia Asemic and Concrete Poetry Exhibition in Rome; Asemic Writing off line & in the Gallery at Minnesota Center for book art in USA; Muestra Latinoamericana de Poesia Visual Hotel Dada in the Museum of Contempary Art of Junin, Argentina; Asemic Tech Exhibit in Barcelona, Spain; and L'Aquila concrete and asemic exhibition in Italy, Arte in Dimora-Discovery of Urban Sites, Italy.

Also, I have been published in many of the major, influential visual poetry journals such as Berenice, Utsanga, Angry Old Man Magazine, Frequenze Poetiche, Dialogue, Angel House Press, Experiment 0, Brave New Word Magazine, Hotel Dada Magazine, Aura Poesia Visual, and Women Asemic Artists & Visual Poets // WAAVe Global as well as blogs including Michael Jacobson's Asemic: The New Post Literate: a Gallery of Asemic Writing , Marco Giovenale's Differx_it, and De Villo Sloan's Asemic Front.

Collaboration has been a fundamental piece in my development as an artist, helping me to learn more about art through interacting with other artists' techniques, values, and knowledge. Engaging in a process of visual communication with another, or with others, has no equivalent experience in art. Space and time stop to initiate a transcendental understanding between souls. Mirroring the deepest and most mysterious processes of language, our daily existence is transformed into signs and glyphs. In this experience, what is "mine" becomes ours; it is a reassuring, humanizing process that unites us. Collaboration has convinced me, too, that artistic creation is not just the domain of a few who possess special knowledge and skill. The page, the pencil and the canvas are no-one's intellectual property. Everyone who seeks to participate can and should.

Kind thanks to all who have collaborated during my art process. Whether you are a co-creator or a viewer, your involvement is a pleasure and an honor for me.

Laura Ortiz, August 2021.

Unwritings

Made in the USA
Las Vegas, NV
21 February 2024